How to
Avoid
the
Evil Eye

How to Avoid the Evil Eye

Brenda Z. Rosenbaum and Stuart Copans

ST. MARTIN'S PRESS   NEW YORK

Design by Laura Hough

Library of Congress Cataloging in
Publication Data

Rosenbaum, Brenda.
    How to avoid the evil eye.

    1. Jews—Folklore. 2.
Superstition—Religious
aspects—Judaism. I. Title.
GR98.R64   1985   398'.089924   85–1772
ISBN 0-312-39584-1 (pbk.)

First Edition

10 9 8 7 6 5 4 3 2 1

For Paul
and
For Mary

Contents

"My mother had two favorite sayings: one was 'Only peasants are superstitious,' and the other was '*kinahora*' [no Evil Eye]."

"If it's good luck to break a wineglass, I wonder what happens with a punch bowl?"

"Isn't there a charm for preventing twins?"

"Drawing a circle around the mother and newborn protects them from harm."

"It's certainly a lot cheaper than Blue Cross/Blue Shield."

"How can we name the baby after Uncle Moshe? He's not dead."

"With Uncle Moshe who can tell the difference?"

Acknowledgments

Thank you to:

William Novak for generously sharing his time and expertise;

Rabbi Harold Kushner for his gracious support;

Paul Rosenbaum for his unstinting computer assistance;

Mary Copans for her patience and encouragement;

Helen Rees, our agent, for her persistence;

Brandeis University's Goldfarb Library and the American Jewish Historical Society for use of their excellent collections of Judaica;

and

All the *bubbes* and *zaydes* down through the generations.

Preface

How to Avoid the Evil Eye is a humorously illustrated collection of Jewish superstitions. It includes superstitions both of Jewish origin and those that were borrowed from neighboring cultures (German, Polish, Russian, Middle Eastern) but through adaptation and modification have come to be identified with Jewish people. The collection covers a period that dates back to the Talmud, but draws mainly from the eighteenth and nineteenth centuries. The collection, more Ashkenazïc than Sephardic, deals with superstitions attached to daily life—its crises, anxieties, passages—times of change, and times of vulnerability. It is an attempt to recollect a very human part of our Jewish heritage—namely, how our parents and grandparents coped with the fears of their day—through the use of whimsical cartoons that place the old superstitions in a contemporary context.

We believe that people like to remember their families' peculiar *bubbemeysas* (old wives' tales). They seem to be tickled to learn that other families had the same ones—or even some that were more bizarre. As children of the age of psychiatry, we are intrigued by the methods our grandparents used to explain the unexplainable. And perhaps there is a part of us that believes the admonition of the Hasidic rebbes in the *Sefer Hasidim*: "One should not believe in superstitions, but still it is best to be heedful of them."

1.
How to Avoid the Evil Eye

The hand is used to banish the Evil Eye. When a husband gives the Evil Eye to his wife (or vice versa), she need only open her hand and say "*hamesh*" ("five") and the Evil Eye will be removed.

To avoid the Evil Eye, any complimentary comment must immediately be followed by the declaration *"kein ayin hara"* ("no evil eye").

To hide good fortune from the Evil Eye, one avoids mentioning the date of a birthday or the exact age of a person.

If a person does mention his age, to protect himself he adds, *"biz hindert un tzvantzig"* ("until a hundred and twenty," the age of Moses when he died).

To divert the glance of the Evil Eye, interesting objects may be hung between the eyes of the endangered person.

Protection from the Evil Eye can be gained by wearing an amulet inscribed with *shemoth* (names): the name of God, certain angels, and biblical quotations.

Genesis 49:22, which appears frequently on amulets, is believed to be effective against the Evil Eye. It reads: "Joseph is a fruitful vine, a fruitful vine by a fountain." The word for "vine" (*ayin*) is also the Hebrew word for "eye."

15

A piece of bread and salt or Passover matzoh is put into the pockets of particularly beautiful children to protect them from the Evil Eye.

Praising a child will attract the Evil Eye. Therefore one must say of a beautiful child, "She is so homely."

Enumerating people or wealth can provoke the Evil Eye. The proper counting of children is : *"Nit eyns, nit zvei, nit drei"* ("Not one, not two, not three").

As protection against the Evil Eye, especially in the case of children, the Havdalah candle is lit, placed in front of the child's open mouth, and then put out so that the smoke can enter.

18

Praising a baby or boasting about him is an invitation to the Evil Eye.

To counteract the Evil Eye, dip the hem of a child's garment in wine and wipe his face with it or put garlic in his ear.

Since fish live beneath the surface of the water and cannot be seen, they are immune to the effects of the Evil Eye. (Talmud. Ber. 20a). Therefore, their representation on an amulet is effective.

Here is an antidote for the Evil Eye: Take a handful of salt and pass it around the head of the bewitched child, throw a little of it in each corner of the room, and the remainder over the threshold.

If a girl is too pretty, people will be jealous and give her the Evil Eye. A touch of ashes on her forehead spoils the beauty and deters the Evil Eye.

Wearing a piece of coral will protect a young boy from the Evil Eye.

Vows and curses are to be avoided because they might come to pass.

Sisters should not marry on the same day lest the Evil Eye fall on the parents.

Saying things backwards will fool the Evil Eye. To mention the Evil Eye, call it "*git oyg,*" the good eye.

The "fig" gesture, a phallic symbol represented by the thumb thrust out between the first and second fingers, will repel the Evil Eye.

When a mother fears her child may be under the power of the Evil Eye, she licks or kisses the child's forehead three times, spitting after each time. Saliva, a potent life-fluid, drives evil away.

To avert the Evil Eye, spit three times on your fingertips and each time make a quick movement in the air with your hand.

It is customary to spit after a person who is thought to have an evil influence.

2.
Marriage

To combat evil spirits, it is best to pretend that the wedding day is a day of mourning rather than a day of joy. Therefore, there is fasting and much loud weeping.

Mourning, Schmourning! If you knew my future son-in-law you'd be weeping too!

A glass is broken at the wedding ceremony to appease or to frighten away evil spirits.

Because demons lurk in the darkness, weddings are brightly lit with torches and candles.

In places where it is thought that evil spirits are vulnerable to the sound of cutting, a relative is stationed in the synagogue to cut paper or cloth for the duration of the wedding ceremony.

During an epidemic, if a marriage takes place in the cemetery, the cholera will somehow be conducted down into the grave. The marriage of orphans or the lame in this circumstance is particularly efficacious.

The bride or groom circles the other under the *chuppah* three or seven times because a closed circle is believed to repel demons.

Prior to the wedding day, both the bride and groom are protected from evil spirits waiting to disrupt the happy event. The bride is secluded, and the groom may not venture out alone.

Throwing rice, raisins, nuts, and almonds at the bridal pair insures fertility.

It is good luck to help a marriage along or play host at a wedding.

Breaking dishes when an engagement is announced frightens off evil spirits that are attracted by a joyous event.

Tuesday is thought to be an auspicious day for a wedding because in Genesis God says of the third day "It was good" twice, while of the other days this phrase is mentioned only once. Likewise, Monday is unlucky because it is not mentioned at all.

At the end of a wedding ceremony, the bride and groom attempt to step on one another's feet. The one who succeeds is assured of dominance in their life together.

Somehow I don't think they're going to have an easy marriage.

3.
Pregnancy

Pregnancy may be induced by the sight of the ritual knife used for circumcision, or by drinking water from a bowl placed under the "Chair of Elijah" during the ceremony.

Eating eggs, hens, or fish to break the fast after the marriage ceremony is an inducement to fertility.

If a woman is childless, she should find an *etrog* after Succoth and bite the tip of it.

What a woman sees when she leaves the *mikvah* prior to having sexual relations will influence the child about to be conceived. If she sees a dog, the child will be ugly; if she sees an ass, the child will be stupid; but if she sees a scholar, the child will be brilliant.

No visible preparation is made for an expected baby, because evil spirits would take notice. Every effort is made to keep the birth from their attention.

If a pregnant woman looks upon a deformed person, her unborn child can be affected adversely.

A pregnant woman must not visit a cemetery lest she or her unborn child be contaminated in some way.

A pregnant woman should not step over ropes for fear that the baby will become entangled within her and die.

A miscarriage can be prevented by tying red threads around the throat of the mother.

Women can induce conception by washing their hands and face in water mixed with the sap of an apple tree.

APPLE
TREE   SAP

4.
Birth

A woman's labor will be eased if she is wrapped in the band ordinarily used to secure the Torah.

The more people who know of a woman's labor, the harder will be the delivery.

To alleviate a difficult labor, a long string can be tied from the ark in the synagogue to the lying-in bed.

Birth can be eased by opening all chests, closets, and doors in the house.

To ease labor, the expectant mother can eat leftover *afikomen* or chew the *pitom* of an *etrog*.

Kaporot performed in the birthing room will ease labor. It is thought that the hen will expiate the mother's sins, as well as scare away the demons that are causing pain.

Because evil spirits cannot penetrate a closed circle, a woman is led around a table three times in order to ease birth.

Blowing the shofar in the room of a woman in labor will frighten away the demons.

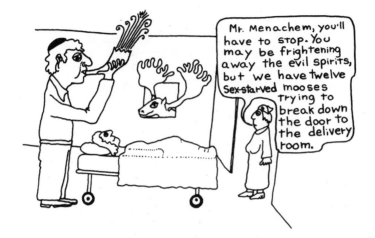

During childbirth, some of the husband's garments are laid on his wife's bed so that demons will jump into them rather than enter the body of the mother or child.

Protection in childbirth can be achieved by having a Torah carried to the door of the lying-in room.

To announce the sex of a child before the delivery of the placenta is considered unlucky and is strictly avoided.

After a birth, the umbilical cord and placenta are buried in the earth, where no malign influence can reach them.

Chicken soup bones fed to a new mother are saved and put into a sieve. The woman in childbed has not recuperated until the sieve is filled.

Lighting a candle in the delivery room will deter evil spirits from entering.

Because demons flee from the sight of iron, successful childbirth can be assured by placing a piece of iron in the bed or under the pillow of a woman in labor.

To avoid binding spells, which can complicate labor, all knots, ties, and buttons on the garments of the woman giving birth are undone.

To protect a woman who has just given birth, draw a circle around the bed.

To safeguard a newborn against being snatched by Lilith—Adam's revengeful, mythic first wife—an amulet inscribed with the names of the protective angels is hung in the lying-in room.

5.
Naming

A child will exhibit some of the attributes of his name-sake, so naming him after a learned person is desirable and naming him after a weak person or failure is avoided.

To be complete, a living person needs his name; there-fore, it is dangerous to take it from him by giving it to a newborn child.

It is bad luck for a bride to have the same name as her mother-in-law, or the groom his father-in-law, because their children cannot then be named after their grand-parents.

Naming a child after a living relative is dangerous because harm, sickness, or death meant for the older person could befall the child.

Entry into heaven could be delayed if an individual is unable to give her Hebrew name to the Angel of Death.

It is necessary to use one's Hebrew name for prayers because angels only understand Hebrew.

The naming of a newborn child after a strong beast such as a lion (*Aryeh*) or bear (*Dov*) could transfer the strength of the animal to the infant and frighten away evil spirits.

If a family has lost a child in infancy, it is best to keep the name of a new baby secret until the child passes through the critical time.

It is best not to disclose the name of a new baby boy before the *bris*, because if he cannot be identified by name, the evil spirits will be defeated in their attempts to harm him.

Because one's name determines one's fate, it is bad luck to name a child after a person who died young, childless, or violently, unless paired with another name of one who lived a long life, had many children, or died peacefully.

The Talmud indicates that changing the name of a sick person will divert the Angel of Death.

It is unwise for several families with a common name to live in the same dwelling lest ill luck befall the wrong person.

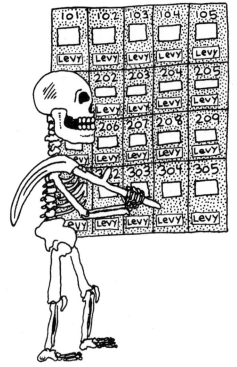

6.
The New Baby

When a baby is born, sugar and candy are put into the carriage to sweeten the life of the child.

To protect an infant, a red ribbon or an amulet is fastened to its clothing. Girl babies may wear tiny gold earrings, perhaps set with turquoise for additional protection.

If a woman has lost several children, the names of succeeding children are designed to trick the Angel of Death. In such cases the baby may be called "*Alteh*" ("old one") or "*Chaim*" ("life").

Evil spirits lie in wait for the *mohel* on the evening before a circumcision. Therefore he should not travel alone, especially at night.

A table set with food on the night before a circumcision serves as a good luck offering to the spirits.

The circumcision knife is regarded as an effective weapon against demons and is often kept under the mother's pillow throughout the night before circumcision.

Sometime before a child is born, the angel Raphael teaches it all the languages of the world, but as the child leaves its mother's womb, the angel gives the child a blow on the upper lip, causing it to forget them all.

If children fall and are not hurt, they fall on invisible pillows that angels place under them.

When a new baby is bathed for the first time, relatives throw coins into the tub so that the child will be rich. Afterwards, the money is given to the midwife.

During the first week of life there is special danger from the Evil Eye. Nobody is supposed to look at the child except the mother, father, and midwife. But if they do they must spit three times and say, "No Evil Eye."

If a baby has been frightened, melted wax can be thrown into the bathwater to determine the cause. The shape the wax takes (usually a dog) will tell the tale.

The tub in which a new baby is bathed for the first time should be one in which children who grew up strong and healthy were bathed.

If the new baby is a boy, the *melamed* brings a *minyan* of boys to recite the Shema every evening of the first week in order to keep demons from the room.

At the celebration after the birth of a male child, beans and peas are served because they are believed to be an effective charm against the spirits and demons that might harm the child.

7.
Childhood

If a child's hair is cut before he can speak, he might remain dumb.

If you step over a child, it will stop growing. To reverse the process, cross back over again.

If a child plays with fire, he will become a bedwetter.

If a child throws food behind himself, he threatens his parents' well-being.

If a child plays with his shadow, it will make him stupid.

Put a key under a child's pillow so he may be as strong as iron; put a prayer book under his pillow to ward off disease.

A boy should not be fed scraps from a pot, for he will lose his memory.

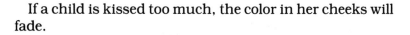

If a child is kissed too much, the color in her cheeks will fade.

If a child sticks out his tongue at a mirror, it will fall off.

A child cannot be carried through a window without danger. She must be carried back through the same window or she will not grow.

If a child laughs in its sleep, it is said to be playing with the Angel of Death; therefore, it should be lightly tapped on the mouth.

Children should not wear black, since it is the color of mourning.

Because evil spirits prey on the souls of little boys, a boy's hair is allowed to grow until he is three years old so that he will be indistinguishable from little girls, who are disregarded by the spirits.

A dying child may be released from death's grasp if nominally sold by his parents for a sheckel.

8.
House and Food

Before moving into a new home, bread and salt should be brought in—bread, so that food may never be lacking, and salt, to secure against evil spirits.

Salt, the miraculous age-old preservative, will drive demons away from the dinner table.

Drink no froth, for it gives cold in the head; nor blow it away, for that gives headaches; nor get rid of it otherwise, for that brings poverty; but wait until it subsides. (Talmud.Hul.105b)

One should not whistle in a house for fear of summoning evil spirits.

Nothing should be removed from the house on Saturday night: a new week should begin full.

It is bad luck to move to a lower floor in the same building.

A garment being worn should not be sewn unless the person chews on a piece of thread; otherwise, the good sense of the individual might be sewn up as well.

Floors should not be swept after someone leaves the house, because this is the customary procedure after someone dies.

One should not drink from or wash in a broken vessel, for spirits may lurk therein.

If you sit on the floor of a house, you will soon be seated there in mourning.

9.
The Body

If a young girl drinks Havdalah wine, she will grow whiskers on her chin or hair on her chest.

Washing of hands is not only for cleanliness but for removing traces of contact with evil spirits.

Itching of the feet implies you will come to some unknown place.

A high, broad brow is the sign of a wise person.

Fingernails should be cut in a certain order. Any change may result in a calamity such as poverty or forgetfulness.

Fingernails that are clipped must then be burned so that after death one need not wander about trying to find them.

If the right eye itches, you will rejoice; if the left, you will cry.

It is bad luck to point with a finger; use a closed hand instead.

10.
Religion and Learning

The loud blasts of the *shofar* are useful in driving away evil spirits.

It is dangerous to leave a book open and go away, for a demon will take your seat and create chaos.

Demons cause fatigue in the knees and wearing out of the clothes of scholars. (Talmud.Ber.6a)

It is thought that the day of a *yahrtzeit* is an unlucky day for any enterprise.

It is lucky to be the tenth of a *minyan*.

It is good luck to make a hole in the *afikomen* and hang it up as a charm in the synagogue or home.

While a mezuzah is a religious object, it is believed by some to have the power of an amulet to bring good luck and ward off misfortune.

A visitor to a synagogue should not be refused an *aliyah*: he may be Elijah.

Eating honey on the New Year is a good omen for a sweet year.

Demons are more powerful than usual just before the departure of Shabbat. Therefore it is dangerous to drink water, which is easily contaminated, before Havdalah.

Only one set of candles should be lit in a house on Shabbat.

If a man reads incorrectly from the Torah, some misfortune may befall the community. For this reason, a practiced Torah reader is desirable.

If you tell a lie on Shabbat, you will die.

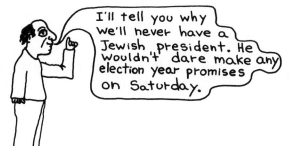

11.
Money

Hanging up a basket of food causes poverty, for he who suspends his food suspends his sustenance. (Talmud. Pes.111b)

In taking money out of a purse or a safe, never remove all of it. Leave a coin or two for luck.

Breadcrumbs thrown on the floor bring poverty. (Talmud.Pes.111b)

Havdalah wine touched to one's pocket will bring good business during the coming week.

Itching of the nose forebodes a quarrel, but itching of the palm indicates that money will be received.

Poverty may be visited on the first tenant in a new house, so it is best not to build a house where none has stood before. If you do, find someone else to live in it for the first year.

If the tablecloth is not removed from the table on Saturday night, creditors will come to collect.

12.
Night

It is best to avoid the synagogue at night, because ghosts of the dead assemble there.

A person is forbidden to give greeting to anyone in the nighttime for fear that it might be a demon. (Talmud. Sanh.44a)

Most people get sick at night, while they're asleep, because they are more susceptible to attack when they're not vigilant.

Because spirits dwell at night, liquids left standing overnight must not be consumed.

A person who drinks from rivers or pools at night is in danger of blindness. (Talmud. Pes. 112a)

Foods placed under a bed for safekeeping during the night are contaminated and no longer fit for consumption.

13.
Dreams

If you go to sleep hungry, you will dream of beggars.

If a dream is forgotten and the dreamer wishes to recall it, let him reverse his undergarment and go back to sleep. He will have the same dream again.

To prevent a bad dream, put a prayer book under your pillow.

If you wake someone who is walking in his sleep, he will die.

A dream of a scroll in the ark foretells death.

Bad dreams can be forgotten by spitting three times after waking in the morning.

It is unwise to tell your dream to a fool. He might interpret it in an unfavorable way and this interpretation can come to pass.

Fasting prevents a bad dream from coming true.

14.
Women

If a girl chews on the bone of the Paschal Lamb at the seder, she will marry within the year.

If a Jewish girl gnaws on bones, she will get a fair-complexioned husband.

A woman should not bake during her monthly period because the cakes won't rise.

If a daughter wears her mother's jewelry while her mother is still living, misfortune will befall the mother.

Women are dangerous to meet after they have been in contact with the dead. (Talmud. Ber.51a)

When a young girl menstruates for the first time, she should be slapped in the face by her mother so that blood will rush to her cheeks, making them rosy forever.

Neither a pregnant woman nor a menstruating woman should enter a cemetery.

A menstruating woman must not touch pickles, wine, or borscht, or they will not keep. Nor should she water plants, for they will die.

15.
Travel

It is wise to carry a portion of *afikomen* on an ocean voyage because a piece of it thrown into a stormy sea will calm the waves.

If a traveler is given *tzedakah* to distribute at his destination, chances for a safe journey are greatly enhanced.

For safety on a journey, the traveler should wear on his garment a needle that has been used to sew a white shroud.

Once a man sets out on a journey, he must not reenter his house if he has forgotten something. He should stand outside and ask to have it handed to him. Otherwise, the forces of the outside world might come into the home, and with them, bad luck.

A man walking alone is in peril from demons, so a traveler should be accompanied part of the way on his journey. His companion should not turn back until the wayfarer can no longer be seen.

16.
Animals

Anyone who eats food nibbled by a mouse is likely to have a poor memory. How much more would this be true of a cat, which consumes the mouse itself? (Talmud.Hor.13a)

Since it is not auspicious to be the first one buried in a cemetery, sometimes a rooster is killed and buried there first.

Swinging a fowl around the head on Yom Kippur is thought to transfer one's sins to the animal, as well as to placate or drive away evil spirits.

77

If an animal is rocked in a cradle before a baby is put in for the first time, any mishap intended for the child will be transferred to the animal.

Fish arouse amorousness and are therefore recommended to be eaten on Friday night.

17.
Health and Illness

During an epidemic, children should wear red ribbons on the wrist or around the neck.

I know it will keep me healthy, Mother — but I have an important trial today and I think it might make it harder to impress the jury.

To make a sick child well, multiply the age of the child by the number *18* (*chai*/life) and give the money to charity.

A seriously ill child is measured with thread, which is taken to a candlemaker, who will use it to make wicks for candles to be donated to the synagogue.

Because the moon causes illness, an infant should not be exposed to moonlight before he cuts his first tooth.

If a child's illness is not caused by the Evil Eye, it is caused by worms.

If women gossip about an invalid in the presence of children, the ailment can be visited upon the youngsters.

If a child is sick, giving the equivalent of his weight in bread or money to the poor will make him well.

He who sneezes during prayer should regard it as a bad omen. (Talmud. Ber.24b)

To keep evil spirits away in times of epidemic, hang white onions and garlic on all the windows and doors and on each of the four walls of every room in the house.

Preventive measures against cholera include hanging a loaf of bread and a bottle of rose water in the house while reciting Psalm 27:5.

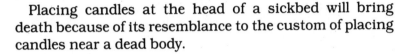

Placing candles at the head of a sickbed will bring death because of its resemblance to the custom of placing candles near a dead body.

When a person is sick, others must not gossip about his sins.

News of serious illness is withheld for three days lest the spirits cause the premature death of the invalid after overhearing talk of his weakened condition.

If an old woman goes to the cemetery, puts a shawl on the grave of a pious relative, and then places it under the pillow of a sick person, the patient will recover.

Spilled Havdalah wine daubed on the eyelids is a cure for weak eyesight.

If a parchment amulet is used to prevent illness, it must be wrapped in clean leather and hung about the neck of the recipient without his knowledge, or while he is asleep, and he is not to look at it for the next twenty-four hours.

Never eat or laugh behind the back of your fellow man. You may injure his health.

18.
Death

Mentioning the Angel of Death will attract his attention.

Rain on the day of a funeral is a sign of compassion and forgiveness toward the dead.

Wearing black is unlucky because it is a sign of death in the family.

A dead body should not be left alone, for evil spirits wandering about may enter it.

If a living person is mentioned in the same breath as a dead person, a protective phrase must be added, such as "May he live to be a hundred and twenty."

One should not drink out of the glass of a mourner, or borrow his possessions during the shiva period, in case the mourner is contaminated by contact with the spirit world.

Garlic is taken to the cemetery in order to drive away demons that seek to attach themselves to visitors.

After a funeral, the procession homeward may stop three or seven times (sometimes coupled with recitations of psalms) in order to confuse and shake off the evil spirits that follow.

The longest route is always taken to the cemetery for a burial. Some say it is out of love and the wish to delay the final parting; others say it is so that the ghost of the deceased will lose its way if it tries to return.

One should not visit the same grave twice in one day.

After attending a funeral, people must wash their hands before reentering their homes in order to avoid contamination by demons, who follow the dead and hover around their graves.

If a grave has been dug, it cannot be left uncovered overnight lest another death occur in the community within a few days.

Bending the fingers of a dead man to form the Hebrew letters of *Shaddai* (Almighty) will fend off demons.

When a person leaves a cemetery, he plucks some blades of grass and throws them behind his back, perhaps to repel the demons that lurk behind.

The clothes of the dead must be free from knots and loops so that the soul will be free to leave the body.

He may have worn doubleknits in life, but in death he'll have to wear his plain wool suit.

In a house where someone has died, mirrors are covered so that the spirit of the dead cannot take away any living soul exposed in the mirror, and so that the spirit of the dead cannot itself linger within the shiny surface.

The coffin should precede the living out of the house so that the spirits will leave with it, thereby preventing them from seizing another victim.

A pebble is put on the grave after a visit to the cemetery so that the soul won't come out and follow you home.

The pouring out of all water in and near a house where death has occurred is a silent announcement of death, which is dangerous to mention aloud.

The way and day a person dies is thought to be a good or bad omen for the deceased. To die amid laughter or on Shabbat eve is a good omen; to die amid weeping or at the close of Shabbat is a bad omen. (Talmud. Ket.103b)

The custom of the bereaved changing seats in the synagogue is thought to provide a disguise for the mourner who may have been contaminated by contact with the spirit world.

To discover whether husband or wife will die first, calculate the numerical value of the letters in the name of each. If the number is even, the man will die first; if odd, the woman.

The windows of the room in which a person is dying should be opened to allow the soul to depart. Afterwards, the window must be shut immediately lest Death or some other demon return.

Removal of a feather pillow from beneath the head of a dying person helps the soul to depart more easily. The iron keys of the synagogue, if placed under the pillow, have the same effect.

A person dies when he has used up the number of words allotted to him in his lifetime.

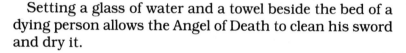

Setting a glass of water and a towel beside the bed of a dying person allows the Angel of Death to clean his sword and dry it.

. . . and one for good luck!

Glossary

afikomen: Pieces of matzoh hidden during the Passover seder and later eaten at the end of the meal. Children traditionally find the pieces and bargain with the head of the household for their return so that the meal may be completed.

aliyah: Ascent to the Torah to read a portion or recite the blessings before and after the reading. It is considered an honor.

alteh: Old one.

aryeh: Lion.

Ashkenazi: Referring to the Jews of Germany and Eastern Europe.

ayin: Eye.

biz hindert un tzvantzig: Until one hundred and twenty.

bris: Circumcision ceremony performed on the eighth day after the birth of a boy.

bubbemeysas: Old wives' tales.

chaim: Life.

chuppah: The canopy under which the bride and groom stand during their wedding.

dov: Bear.

etrog: A citrus fruit similar to the lemon; used on the Succoth holiday as one of the symbols of the harvest.

Evil Eye: A glance of envy or anger considered capable of inflicting harm.

git oyg: Good eye.

hamesh: Five.

Hasidic: A word meaning "pious," describing followers of Hasidism, a religious movement founded in eighteenth-century Poland.

Havdalah: A ceremony held at the conclusion of the Sabbath; a long, braided candle is lit and blessings are made over wine and spices.

kinahora: A popular contraction of *kein ayin hara*, literally, "no Evil Eye."

kaporot: Vicarious atonement; passing a rooster around the head of a person whose sins are thereby passed on to the animal. In places where kaporot is still practiced, coins are more often substituted for the scapegoat animal.

matzoh: Unleavened bread eaten during Passover to remind the Jewish people of their hasty exodus from Egypt.

melamed: Hebrew teacher.

mikvah: A ritual purification bath.

menchlichkeit: The state of being a "mench," a responsible, decent human being.

minyan: A quorum of ten adult Jews (Orthodox Jews specify males) required to perform certain religious rites.

mohel: The man who performs the ritual of circumcision.

Moshiach: The Messiah.

Nit eyns, nit zvei, nit drei: Not one, not two, not three.

Paschal Lamb: The lamb sacrificed at the time of the Exodus, represented on the seder plate by a lamb shank bone.

Pirke Aboth: "Ethics of the Fathers," a tractate of the Talmud that elaborates on ethical maxims of the Talmudic sages.

pitom: The stem of the etrog.

Reden zie nit 'iddish?: Don't you speak Yiddish?

Rosh Hashanah: The Jewish New Year.

seichel: Intelligence, common sense.

Sephardic: Referring to Jews from Spain and Portugal and the Jewish communities of the Middle East.

Shabbat: The seventh day of the week; a holy day of rest and abstention from work.

Shaddai: One of the names of God: "Almighty."

Shema: The first word of the prayer "Hear, O Isreal, The Lord our God, the Lord is One." (Deut. 6:4)

shemoth: Names.

Shmoneh Esrey: The eighteen benedictions that constitute the central part of the daily prayer service; also referred to as the Amidah.

shofar: A hollowed ram's horn blown on certain ritual ocasions, particularly Rosh Hashanah and Yom Kippur.

Succoth: An autumn harvest holiday recalling the forty-year period after the Exodus when the Jewish people lived in the wilderness in tents or booths.

Torah: The first five books of the Hebrew Bible; the sacred text is inscribed on a parchment scroll for reading at prescribed times.

tzedakah: Fulfillment of one's charitable obligations.

yahrtzeit: The anniversary of the death of a family member.

Bibliography

Bermant, Chaim. *The Walled Garden.* New York: Macmillan Publishing Co., Inc., 1974.

Cohen, Rev. Dr. A. *Everyman's Talmud.* New York: E.P. Dutton & Co., 1949.

Dantzker, S. "Some Jewish Folk Habits and Superstitions," *New York Folklore Quarterly,* XIV, No. 2 (Summer, 1938).

Encyclopedia Judaica. Jerusalem: Keter Publishing House Ltd., 1971.

Feldman, W. M. *The Jewish Child.* London: Tindall & Cox, 1917.

Finesinger, Sol B. "The Shofar," *Hebrew Union College Annual,* VIII–IX (1931–32), 193–228.

Gaster, Theodore H. *Customs and Folkways of Jewish Life.* New York: Wm. Sloan Associates, 1955.

The Jewish Encyclopedia. New York: Ktav Publishing House, Inc., 1901.

Kaganoff, Benzion C. *A Dictionary of Jewish Names and Their History.* New York: Schocken Books, 1977.

Kolatch, Alfred J. *The Jewish Book of Why.* New York: Jonathan David Publishers, Inc., 1981.

Lauterbach, Jacob Z. "The Ceremony of Breaking Glass at Weddings," *Hebrew Union College Annual,* II (1925), 351–380.

——————. "The Naming of Children in Jewish Folklore, Ritual and Practice," *Central Conference of American Rabbis Yearbook,* XLII (1932), 316–360.

Magic and Superstition in the Jewish Tradition. Chicago: Spertus College of Judaica Press, 1975.

Maloney, Clarence (ed.). *The Evil Eye.* New York: Columbia University Press, 1976.

Marcus, Jacob R. *The Jew in the Medieval World.* New York: Harper & Row, Publishers, 1938.

Mintz, Jerome R. *Legends of the Hasidim*. Chicago: University of Chicago Press, 1968.

Moss, Leonard W., and Applebaum, Emanuel. "Folklore Among Detroit Jews," *Michigan Jewish History*, III, No. 3 (June 1963), 2–9.

Myerhoff, Barbara. *Number Our Days*. New York: Simon and Schuster, 1978.

Pollack, Herman. *Jewish Folkways in Germanic Lands, 1948–1806*. Cambridge, Massachusetts: M.I.T. Press, 1971.

Rappoport, Dr. Angelo S. *The Folklore of the Jews*. London: The Soncino Press, 1937.

Roskies, Diane K., and Roskies, David G. *The Shtetl Book*. New York: Ktav Publishing House, Inc., 1975.

Schauss, Hayyim. *Guide to Jewish Holy Days: History and Observance*. New York: Schocken Books, 1962. (First published in 1938.)

──────. *The Lifetime of a Jew*. Cincinnati: Union of American Hebrew Congregations, 1950.

Schrire, Theodore. *Hebrew Magic Amulets: Their Decipherment and Interpretation*. New York: Behrman House, Inc., 1982.

Siegel, Richard, and Rheins, Carl (eds.). *The Jewish Almanac*. New York: Bantam Books, Inc., 1980.

Talmage, Frank (ed.). *Studies in Jewish Folklore*. Proceedings of a Regional Conference of the Association for Jewish Studies. Held at Spertus College of Judaica, Chicago, May 1–3, 1971. Cambridge, Massachusetts: Association for Jewish Studies, 1980.

Trachtenberg, Joshua. *Jewish Magic and Superstition: A Study in Folk Religion*. New York: Behrman House, Inc., 1939.

Yoffie, Leah Rachel. "Popular Beliefs and Customs Among the Yiddish-Speaking Jews of St. Louis, Missouri," *Journal of American Folklore*, XXXVIII, No. 149 (July–Sept. 1925), 375–399.

Zborowski, Mark, and Herzog, Elizabeth. *Life is With People: The Culture of the Shtetl*. New York: Schocken Books, 1952.